For Mom and Dad, thank you for everything,
and for Ezra, thanks for the history lessons

Farrar Straus Giroux Books for Young Readers • An imprint of Macmillan Publishing Group, LLC • 120 Broadway, New York, NY 10271
mackids.com • Copyright © 2022 by Sally Deng. All rights reserved. • Our books may be purchased in bulk for promotional, educational, or
business use. Please contact your local bookseller or the Macmillan Corporate and Premium Sales Department at (800) 221-7945 ext. 5442 or
by email at MacmillanSpecialMarkets@macmillan.com. • Library of Congress Cataloging-in-Publication Data is available. • First edition, 2022
Printed in China by Toppan Leefung Printing Ltd., Dongguan City, Guangdong Province
ISBN 978-0-374-38838-6 (hardcover) • 10 9 8 7 6 5 4 3 2 1

The art for this book was created using acrylic paint and colored pencils on paper. The text was set in Adobe Jenson and
Vineyard Swash Caps, and the display type was set in Elphinstone. Designed by Mercedes Padró, with art direction by Neil Swaab.
Production was supervised by Susan Doran, and the production editor was Helen Seachrist. Edited by Trisha de Guzman.

WARRIOR PRINCESS

The Story of Khutulun

Sally Deng

Farrar Straus Giroux

New York

In the moonlit grasslands of ancient times,
a baby girl took her first breath.
Her father, the khan, cradled her in his arms.

"Here is my daughter, child of the moon," he proclaimed.
"Khutulun, Princess of Mongolia!"

Life in Khutulun's tribe was demanding; she and her fourteen older brothers worked and trained every day. Everything they did would prepare them to become warriors.

"You are the great-great-grandchildren of the *great* Genghis Khan," their father told them.

"You must all do your part."

"Your mother was fearless when she was young!" the khan told his children.

"Back in the day, she would fight soldiers even larger than me!"

"I want to be just like you, Eej!" Khutulun said as she pranced about.

Her mother, the khatun, sometimes brought
Khutulun to her meetings. Although the khan's advisers
often argued, everyone listened when the khatun spoke.

Khutulun was proud of her mother.
But listening to adults squabble was no fun.
She'd rather be outside, where she was free
to go as fast as she wanted on her horse.

Their tribe had a saying:

"*A Mongol without a horse is like a bird without wings.*"

Their children were on horses before they could even walk. For Khutulun, riding was as natural as breathing.

Even though it was usually a boy's responsibility, Khutulun learned to hunt alongside her brothers.

She honed her archery skills while she herded goats and sheep. Every time she caught sight of a reddish-gray streak—

—she'd let an arrow fly quick as lightning.

Khutulun also loved to wrestle. There was only one way to win:
force her opponent to the ground!

At first, Khutulun would only compete against other girls. Then she wrestled boys. Eventually Khutulun would go on to challenge opponents twice her size.

She won

every

single

match.

As she grew older, Khutulun started learning
multiple languages and military strategies.

"Study hard," her mother told her.
"Our people need leaders as well as fighters."

Although she excelled in her lessons,
Khutulun knew in her heart where
she belonged. Every night she
dreamt of being in the
grasslands, galloping
under the infinite sky.

The Mongol Empire was divided—
khans from different clans struggled for power.
The day after her sixteenth birthday,
Khutulun approached her father.
   "I will ride with you into battle," she said.
Her father nodded. "It is time."

War at the front was brutal and punishing. The enemy outnumbered them by the thousands and there was little time for rest.

Khutulun struggled for the right words to lift everyone's spirits.

The drumming of hooves matched the rhythm that thudded in Khutulun's chest. She dashed ahead of her troops before the enemy shot their first arrow.

Khutulun homed in on an enemy soldier like an eagle would on its prey. With a heavy *"RAAAHHH!!"* she looped an arm around his neck and yanked him off his horse.

In a flash, she raced back to her troops
and dropped the man at her father's feet.
Silence. Then . . .

. . . a rousing cry broke out! The invigorated
crowd followed her back into the field,
emerging as victors of the day.

Khutulun quickly gained a loyal following on the battlefield. But she soon had to face another obstacle.

Most women her age stopped fighting so they could get married and run their households. But the princess wanted to follow her own path.

"I will marry whoever defeats me in a wrestling match," she announced. "But they should be prepared to forfeit ten horses when I win."

Countless men stepped up to challenge her, but they all failed miserably. Word spread that their warrior princess's herd had grown to over ten thousand horses.

But people still spoke in hushed voices about her unmarried state.

"People are calling Father weak," her eldest brother muttered. "They think that the khan should be able to control his daughter."

One day, a prince from another clan wagered one thousand horses on his match with the princess.

"He would be a strong ally for our family," her mother said softly.

Khutulun lowered her eyes and agreed to throw the match. There was more at stake than just her future.

On the day of the match, Khutulun stepped slowly out of her ger.
She was back on the battlefield.

Alone.

PHWWAAAAAA! Khutulun felt the familiar rush of energy as she darted forward and grabbed the prince's arms. For every push he gave, she equaled him. She was not going to make his victory easy.

By chance, she tilted her head just so.

The moon shone above her, bold and proud.

The roar of the crowd fell away . . .

Adjusting her grip, she gracefully kicked one leg out behind the prince.

Then, with a tug and fluid twist of her waist . . .

There was no sound except the rustling of wind. The fierce look in her father's eyes would have had mighty warriors cowering. But Khutulun's gaze never wavered.

Finally, a small smile formed on the khan's face.

"You should rest," he said. "We will journey out east soon."

He paused. "Our people need you."

A thunderous roar erupted as the crowd cheered for their princess.

Up on a rocky ledge, Khutulun looked out to the grass steppes
in the horizon.

"You fought bravely, Günj," said a soldier. "We await the day you become khan."
Khutulun turned to her fellow comrade and smiled.

"I only ever wish to be here."

The open lands promised a future of hardships.
Unfazed, Khutulun charged forward.

Author's Note

The story of Khutulun is pieced together from many sources, and a lot of liberty was taken in the retelling of this version.

She was born around 1260 as the great-great-granddaughter of Genghis Khan, the founder of the Mongol Empire. Khutulun was a respected warrior, but she wasn't unique in that respect; many women of her time also participated in sports and fought alongside men. She was her father's favorite child, and he often asked for her advice.

We don't know if anyone ever won her challenge, but one story tells of Abtakul, a man who failed to assassinate Khutulun's father. Abtakul's mother offered to be punished instead, but Abtakul, the loyal son, refused. The khan was so moved by them that he pardoned Abtakul and made him an officer in his army. Khutulun was said to have met Abtakul on the battlefield. They fell in love and eventually married.

Whether or not this was true, Khutulun never stopped fighting. Although her father wanted to name her as his successor, the princess was not interested and instead became commander of his army. Up until the very end, Khutulun lived a life she paved for herself.

Perhaps that is why even after thousands of years, Khutulun's legacy continues to inspire in Mongolia today.

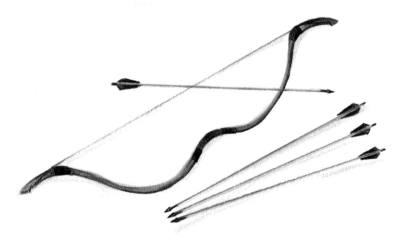

Glossary

eej — Mongolian word for "mother."

Genghis Khan — the founder and first Great Khan of the Mongol Empire.

ger — a round tent used by nomads, or traveling people, as their homes.

günj — Mongolian word for "princess."

khan — Male rulers of ancient Mongolia. Each khan was leader of his own clan. The ruler of the entire Mongol Empire was called the Great Khan.

khatun — The wife of the khan. Khatuns held very powerful political positions in ancient Mongolia.

Khutulun — A Mongolian warrior princess who lived in the mid-1200s. Her name refers to moonlight.

Mongol Empire — Founded in 1206, the Mongol Empire was the largest land empire in history. It stretched from Central Europe to the Korea kingdom and extended from the Arctic down to India.

steppes — large areas of flat, open grassland.